The Weather Box

Ann Weil
Illustrated by Bridget Starr Taylor

Rigby®

A Harcourt Achieve Imprint

www.Rigby.com
1-800-531-5015

Literacy by Design Leveled Readers: *The Weather Box*

ISBN-13: 978-1-4189-3788-1
ISBN-10:   1-4189-3788-6

Printed in China
1A 2 3 4 5 6 7 8 985 13 12 11 10 09 08 07

Contents

Chapter 1

A New Invention

"**W**hat are you doing in here?" Heesoo asked his older brother Woojin. Heesoo had gone into the garage to get out of the pouring rain and found Woojin sitting quietly on the floor with their father's toolbox. "I thought you were playing soccer today."

"My team couldn't play soccer because it's raining," Woojin answered, picking up a screwdriver.

"Is that Dad's old radio, and does he know that you're playing with it?" Woojin and Heesoo's father worked for a company that put cable wires into people's houses and apartments so that people could watch cable television. He often showed the boys how his tools worked.

Woojin nodded and said, "The radio was broken, so Dad said I could have it."

"Did you fix it?" Heesoo asked, looking over Woojin's shoulder. Heesoo knew that Woojin was very good at fixing things, and he liked to watch his older brother work with tools in the garage.

"Maybe," said Woojin. He didn't want to tell his little brother that he was not actually trying to fix the old radio. He was just using its pieces to make his newest invention—a weather box. Tightening the last screw on the cover, he was almost finished.

"This is really another one of your great inventions, isn't it?" Heesoo also knew that his big brother was a good inventor. "What does it do?" Heesoo was so excited that he was jumping up and down, his wet shoes squeaking against the cement floor of the garage.

"It's a weather box," said Woojin, speaking loudly so that Heesoo could hear him over the noise of the rain hitting the tin roof of the garage. "This is the third Sunday in a row that I haven't been able to play soccer because of the rain, so I decided to invent a weather box to control the weather."

"What does this do?" Heesoo asked, reaching for the red button beneath the dial of the weather box.

"Wait, I haven't tested that yet!" Woojin cried out. But it was too late. Heesoo had already pressed the button.

There was a bright flash of light outside the garage, and then Woojin and Heesoo heard a terrible boom, louder than anything either of them had ever heard before.

"What happened?" Heesoo whispered.

Chapter 2

Rain, Rain, Go Away

"**I** think my new invention works," Woojin said slowly. He pointed outside and said, "Look, it actually stopped raining."

Creeping toward the door, Heesoo looked outside and up at the sky. The rain clouds were gone, and the sky was clear blue. The sun was shining so brightly that it was already drying up the huge puddles left by the fierce rainstorm.

"Wow, you did it!" Heesoo cheered, jumping to the doorway so he could stretch out his hand to tell whether the rain had really stopped falling.

"Did what?" asked their father curiously as he walked toward them from the house.

Heesoo ran over to him and jumped into his arms, nearly knocking Dad over and yelling, "Dad, Woojin invented a weather box that can stop the rain!"

"That's nice," Dad said as he put Heesoo back down on the ground. "Heesoo, I'd like you to change out of these wet clothes before dinnertime."

"OK, Dad," Heesoo replied, running toward the house.

Dad looked up at the clear, blue sky and remarked, "Well, look at that. I guess we ended up with nice weather today after all."

Woojin stayed behind in the garage. He didn't want Heesoo to play with his weather box, so he decided to hide it. He thought about bringing it with him to the bedroom he shared with Heesoo, but Heesoo could find it there. He decided to put it back in the exact same spot where his father had stored the radio in the first place, on the crowded shelf in the corner of the garage. Then he put away all the tools he had been using and hurried to the house to wash his hands before dinner.

The rest of his family was just sitting down to eat when Woojin joined them at the dinner table. Woojin was very hungry because he had been working so hard all day that he had forgotten to eat lunch. The fish soup, rice, beef, and vegetable dishes that his mother had cooked for dinner smelled wonderful. Woojin could hardly wait for Dad to take his first bite of food so that the rest of the family could begin eating.

"So what did you do this afternoon?" Mom asked Woojin as she filled her cup from the teapot.

"I was working on one of my new inventions—a weather box!" Woojin answered, then took a small sip of his own drink.

"That sounds interesting," Mom said as she smiled and looked at Dad, who smiled knowingly back at her.

"It was actually very easy to make because all I had to do was . . ." Woojin began to explain, but then Heesoo interrupted him.

"I was playing in some puddles in the backyard," Heesoo said. "Then it started raining harder, so I ran into the garage to get out of the rain. Then all of a sudden Woojin's weather box made the rain stop!"

"It *was* strange that the rain stopped so unexpectedly," Dad said, with a puzzled expression on his face.

Heesoo looked at Woojin to see if Woojin would tell Mom and Dad more about the weather box, but Woojin just put another spoonful of rice in his mouth and chewed thoughtfully. Heesoo wondered if Woojin would tell Mom and Dad more about his invention later, after Heesoo went to bed.

Chapter 3

The Weather Box Is Gone!

The next afternoon on the bus ride home from school, Woojin couldn't stop thinking about his weather box. It had taken extra concentration all day at school to stay focused on the teacher and take notes in class when he really wanted to be back at home working on his exciting new invention.

As soon as the bus came to a stop in front of his house, Woojin jumped out and ran into the garage. But when he looked on the long shelf in the corner of the garage, the weather box wasn't there. Woojin was confused because he was sure that he had put the weather box back on that shelf. Although he clearly remembered doing that, he decided to search the whole garage, just in case. He hoped Heesoo hadn't gone to the garage and taken the weather box without asking him first. Woojin knew his little brother could be very curious sometimes.

Woojin looked on every single shelf in the garage and in several old boxes, but there was no doubt. The weather box was gone!

"Mom, I can't find my weather box!" Woojin called as he took his shoes off by the front door. "I left it on a shelf in the corner of the garage, and now it's missing. Have you seen it?"

"What does it look like?" asked his mother, looking up from the newspaper she was reading.

"It's that old radio, Mom," Heesoo said from where he was playing on the living room floor.

Mom looked at Woojin, thought for a moment, and then said, "Your father was looking for that old radio just this morning."

Suddenly Woojin felt a heavy knot tighten in his stomach as he realized what must have happened: his father had taken the weather box!

Woojin jumped up from the sofa, ran to the hall phone, and called Dad's cell phone. "Please answer the phone, Dad," Woojin said to himself as he listened to the phone ring.

"Hi, Dad, I think you might have taken my weather box by mistake this morning," Woojin said anxiously as Dad answered the phone.

"I can't hear you, son," Dad said, speaking very loudly. "My cell phone isn't working very well today."

"I said, I think you have my weather— I mean, I think you have that old broken radio you gave to me," Woojin said even louder.

"Yes, I saw that you fixed that old radio, and I was just going to turn it on to listen to some music while I work on this job," Dad answered.

"No, Dad, don't use the—"

"Sorry, son, I still can't hear you very well. We'll talk later on tonight when I get home," Dad said as he hung up the phone.

Woojin hung up the hall phone. Dad hadn't used the weather box yet, but what would happen if he did?

"Do you know where Dad's working this afternoon?" he asked his mother as he quickly put his gym shoes back on.

"I think he said that he was putting cable wires into the Senior Citizens' Center on Greentree Road today."

"Thanks, Mom," Woojin called, running outside to get his bike.

"Where are you going?" Mom called after him.

"I'm going to try to find Dad at the Center. I have to talk to him about that radio!" Woojin replied as he put on his bike helmet.

"Can I come with you?" Heesoo begged.

"No, Heesoo, I have to ride really fast and you won't be able to keep up with me," Woojin answered as he jumped on his bike and quickly pedaled away. Woojin had to find Dad before he used the weather box and accidentally changed the weather!

Woojin raced toward the Senior Citizens' Center. He thought he remembered how to get there, but soon all the houses and streets began to look the same. He turned onto Maple Drive, but the street ended in a circle, and suddenly Woojin was lost.

"Woojin, wait for me!"

Woojin turned around at the sound of Heesoo's voice. At first Woojin was bothered that his little brother had followed him after he had specifically told Heesoo not to come. But then he realized that Heesoo might be able to help him. Maybe Heeso remembered how to get to the Center.

"I thought you said you were going to the Senior Citizens' Center," Heesoo said as he stopped his bike next to Woojin's, breathing hard from racing after his brother.

"I'm trying to find it," Woojin said, "but I can't remember where it is."

The Weather Box Is Gone!

Chapter 4

Snow!

Heesoo pointed toward the top of a tall oak tree that stood higher than all of the houses and asked, "Isn't that the tree in the front yard of the Senior Citizens' Center?"

Woojin and Heesoo pedaled toward the tall tree as fast as they could. Soon both boys were sweating from riding their bikes so long and so hard on such a warm day.

"I'm hot, Woojin," Heesoo complained, "and thirsty."

"You can get something to drink later," Woojin said. "Right now we have to go warn Dad about the weather box."

Snow!

Suddenly they saw a bright flash streak across the sky. "Look!" said Heesoo, pointing up at an enormous white cloud forming over the oak tree. With a loud boom, the cloud exploded into thousands of little white flakes.

"It's snowing!" Heesoo yelled excitedly.

They were only a block away from the tall tree when Woojin saw a road sign for the Senior Citizens' Center with an arrow pointing to the right. He followed the sign, made a right turn, and pedaled as quickly as he could down Greentree Road toward the oak tree. He was sure that the weather box had caused the snow. When he looked up at the sky again, he saw that the wet snow was falling even faster and heavier now.

Snow!

Woojin could hear Heesoo huffing and puffing behind him, trying to pedal fast enough to keep up. Then Woojin saw the Center with his father's van parked in the driveway. The van was already surrounded by piles of snow as high as the tires! But where was his father?

"Dad, where are you?" Woojin shouted nervously, as he tried to pedal up the driveway through the snow.

Woojin looked all around the Center and finally found his father trying to shovel the heavy snow away from the side of the building.

"Boys, what are you doing here?" Dad asked.

"I came to help you," Woojin answered, shivering in the sudden cold.

"So did I!" yelled Heesoo, running over to them. He slipped and landed happily in a pile of snow next to Woojin.

"Thanks, boys. I can't believe it's snowing in the middle of summer! I could really use your help with all this shoveling. I need to drill a hole here so I can put a cable wire through this wall, but all of this snow keeps getting in the way. Maybe you can look in the van for something you could use as a shovel," Dad suggested.

Woojin knew that the best thing he could do to help would be to find the weather box and turn its dial back to sunshine. If he didn't, soon the Senior Citizens' Center would be buried under the snow, and so would Dad!

"I can't get any work done in this snowstorm, but this job is important, and I need to finish it today," Dad said, sounding concerned. "I called my boss and told him I was unable to do this job right now because it was snowing. He just laughed and said that was the best joke he had heard all day."

"Where's that old radio, Dad?" Woojin asked, starting to search for it in the huge pile of snow behind Dad.

"You won't be able to hear the weather report on it, Woojin," Dad said. "I tried to listen to some music just before it started to snow, but that old radio is still broken. I left it on the ground next to the van."

Woojin tried to run back down the driveway to where Dad had parked the van, but the snow on the ground was up to his knees now. The cold snow stuck to his legs and made them feel like a pair of icicles, but he kept dragging his feet slowly through the snow, hoping to bump into the weather box.

Finally Woojin's foot hit something hard, and he knelt down and dug through the snow until he uncovered the weather box! He quickly brushed away the snow and tried to turn the dial to sunshine, but the dial wouldn't move. It was frozen!

Woojin began rubbing the weather box with his shirt to help melt the snow and unfreeze the dial. With each passing second, more snow fell, piling up higher and higher around Woojin.

After what felt like hours (even though it was really only a minute or two) Woojin tried again to turn the dial, and it moved! Woojin turned the dial to sunshine and cautiously pressed the button. . . .

Chapter 5

The Sun Returns

Boom!

Woojin looked up and saw that the snow had suddenly stopped falling. He gazed at the thick clouds as they seemed to evaporate into the air and fade out of sight until there was nothing left but bright blue sky.

The warm sun was shining down, and the air was beginning to feel like a hot summer day again. Woojin breathed a huge sigh of relief as the snow around him started to melt.

Heesoo ran over to Woojin, and complained, "My snowman is melting! Can't you make it cold again so it will snow some more? Then I can go sledding and build a snow fort and invite my friends over for a snowball fight . . . "

Woojin just shook his head. Sometimes it was impossible to please everyone.

"It looks like I'll be able to finish this job on time after all," Dad called to the boys as they walked toward him through the melting snow.

"Dad, Woojin stopped the snowstorm!" Heesoo said, but Dad couldn't hear him very well over the noisy drill.

"That's nice," Dad said.

Woojin just smiled. He was already busy planning his next invention: electric pants to keep his legs warm the next time it snowed!